PIANO TEACHING AS A CAREER
Tips And Advice On Becoming A Piano Teacher

ALEXANDRA WESTCOTT, BA

© 2012 Alexandra Westcott. All rights reserved.
ISBN 978-1-4467-6359-9

Index

Introduction

Chapter 1.   Starting Up

Chapter 2.   Getting Going

Chapter 3.   Administration

Chapter 4.   Interviews

Chapter 5.   The Lessons

Chapter 6.   Supporting Activities

Chapter 7.   Additional Motivational pursuits

Chapter 8.   Parental Help

Chapter 9.   Holiday work

Chapter 10. Ending lessons

Appendix i   Recommended books/resources

Appendix ii   Article: Piano Playing and the Alexander Technique

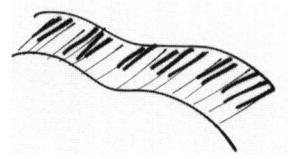

Introduction

I began the piano at about 8 years old, teaching myself using my sister's piano books. My parents had the foresight to ignore that I said I didn't want lessons (my peers all had lessons and hated practicing — I loved it and didn't want that ruined) and I was lucky enough to have an amazing and wonderful man as a teacher who became a lifelong friend until his death some 20 years ago. Although he didn't benefit my technique, he nurtured my enthusiasm with encouragement and love.

Later in life I realized that my playing had reached a plateau. The old adage 'when the pupil is ready the teacher arrives' held good and I met Nelly Ben Or, the leading exponent of utilizing the Alexander Technique in piano playing. At once I could see that this could further my playing. I found her suggestions ridiculously logical (I'm still not sure why we all get ourselves tied in knots for no reason — the human being has some very strange reactions!), and she profoundly affected the way I not only played, but approached both the instrument and the written music.

I had not long prior to meeting Nelly started re-investigating my relationship with the piano and found that I wanted to share my love of music and the instrument with other people. Also to pass on what I was learning from Nelly. I was committed not only to encourage a student's enthusiasm but to do it while engendering a solid technical foundation. The fine line between the two has been a constant challenge ever since!

From only a couple of months into my teaching career I've had between 40 and 50 students a week, and have continually gained insights and feedback from them, and now I'd like to share what I've learnt about the business of teaching itself, both in terms of the practicalities of why and how to get started, to my experiences with the lessons and student themselves.

So you want to teach piano...?

When I started teaching I read copious amounts of material, wanting to be 'the perfect teacher'. It wasn't until I'd actually been teaching for a while that I realized that much of the business of teaching was learned on the job. It is not until you are confronted with the problems that you are forced into finding creative solutions, and this book isn't meant to take away your own learning process.

> *the perfect teacher......*

This little missive cannot replace a solid musical foundation that I'm sure you already have if you are considering teaching as a career.

Neither can it instill the dynamic or vibrant enthusiasm for teaching that is so necessary if you are to be a success. This is what will motivate you to develop your own unique style, to remain patient and optimistic, to remain curious about your students and their individual motivating and learning patterns, and to remain open to new and creative ways to infect your students with your own passion and love for the subject.

What it hopes to do, however, is to prompt you to ask the right questions and make the right choices for yourself when contemplating starting up your business. If I can help you find the path that makes teaching a positive experience for you then I will consider this little book a success.

1. Questions on Starting Up

What is your motivation?

It is a good idea before you start teaching to ask yourself why you want to do it. **It's a wonderfully rewarding job** but has its limitations and frustrations and needs the patience of a saint.

There are certainly some very good practical reasons for teaching – it's usually limited to the school terms and, you can chose your hours (if you become a peripatetic teacher in schools then your hours are obviously limited to those of the school; if you decide to teach children privately then it will NOT be during school hours, and if teaching adults then you have to be flexible; some will be able to come during the day, others will have to come after work). It's incredibly creative and very varied; you will never encounter the same lesson twice, even with the same student.

like working with people

Do you enjoy passing on the things that inspire and interest and enthuse you? In which case you also have to be prepared to be teaching students who have different passions and interests than you! Do you like working with children, or would you prefer to work with adults; they both have different needs and need a different approach. Are you sure you like working with people on such an intimate basis? In a learning situation we all come face to face with our basic fears and foibles and you need to be very understanding. And you need to be able to communicate and to tailor your communication skills appropriately to the age concerned.

Having taught for many years hundreds of wonderful students, I can recommend it highly as challenging and rewarding work. But, teaching is a two way street and it is very difficult, in fact impossible, teaching someone who doesn't want to learn, and herein probably lies the first of the frustrations you can encounter. As I said, you do need patience.

recommend it as highly rewarding work

Who are you teaching?

This sounds a rather redundant question. You want people don't you? ….What I mean is, there are a variety of people out there willing and wanting to learn the piano and its worth asking yourself who would be your perfect student. You may want to teach anyone who enquires, or you may have specific skills on which you want to capitalize. And while the more approaches and styles that you can undertake the better, attracting students who have similar passions to you will lessen frustrations and get you off to a healthy and positive start.

If you teach children, at what age will you start them? **Very young children have very different requirements** and understanding and attention span than those even just a few years older so you need to be geared up to what they can deal with in any one lesson. How you approach each strand of the lesson will be different for each age so you need to have a large number of strategies up your sleeve.

Do you want children of parents who are committed to pursuing the exam route, or do you want to keep it more light-hearted with plenty of pop and jazz and improvising? Although of course these are not mutually exclusive, it will have an impact on the main focus of each lesson.

You may feel that you want to direct your emphasis on the more advanced student, or only on beginners.

Or are adults your speciality? They have varying motivations behind wanting to learn, and some of them have very limited time to commit to playing during the week. But they can be more committed and focussed as they are better aware of *a large number of strategies* what is involved in developing a new skill and this can offset a lack of time.

Once you become more experienced you may well expand your teaching practice to different types of student, but it is worth clarifying your ideas before you start as your answers to these questions will have an impact on your marketing, lesson plans and teaching hours.

As you gain more experience your ideas may change and you adapt accordingly, but for now this gives you a starting point.

Or are adults your speciality?

At the beginning I most enjoyed teaching young beginners. I enjoyed making it as much fun as possible and incorporated them moving and acting and drawing to music in the lesson. I worked hard to build up a close relationship that enabled them to feel safe, take risks, and flower as musicians, and, I have to say, this not only fed their musical creativity, but led to long lasting friendships.

Later on I felt I wanted the challenge of the more advanced student so that we could concentrate on technique and musical style. Needless to say this was also a good incentive for me to keep up the standard of my own playing.

Where do you want to teach? (Home or Away/In Schools)

As a teacher at home you are completely your own boss. This is great in that you can chose how to advertise, what to say on your ads, interview the students (see Chapter 4) and chose those you want to work with. You can choose the hours, policies, fees and conditions without having to adhere to the policy of a school or music studio, and you can arrange the workspace to suit you so that it remains inviting while still professional. (Try and have two piano stools, one of which at least needs to be able to change height, and if possible have a CD player and tape recorder in close proximity to the piano for 'play along' accompaniments or recording exam/performance pieces.)

The drawbacks of working from home are that it can be lonely, and that it can make your home less...homely! You will have people coming in and out every day creating considerable upkeep and cleaning, which you will have to make sure you do when your home is your business space. You will need to have a waiting area for parents, or students who arrive early, and possibly for younger siblings who have to accompany with their parents (though try to discourage this – however well behaved they are, it can get noisy and distracting). On top of all that you have to be disciplined with your work and private hours and sometimes the piano in your home becomes a constant reminder of the frustrations of work, rather than a source of musical pleasure.

> ....drawbacks of working from home

Having said all that, I worked from home as I liked the autonomy, but I made sure I kept in close touch with other local piano teachers, either as close private friends or in support groups, and continued to study in both the teaching and playing fields; this kept me in touch with other like minds with whom I could have lively debate and conversations. I sometimes wished my work wasn't in my home, but for me the benefits way outweighed the drawbacks, and in any case I always took myself out of the house during the day for a coffee or a walk!

If you decide to work in a school then you have set hours outside your home, and hours that can fit with family life if you yourself have children. You go and come from work so that your working and private life remain separate; You have the support of the school and the other teachers, though you most likely will still have to deal with the administration of billing etc; You also come under the auspices of the school and their standards and specific requirements which can be a useful guide and boundary, and you won't have to do your own marketing, or struggle to get business.

Unfortunately you don't have the automatic contact with the parents that you do when they collect their offspring from your house, and I have had many students and parents who have transferred to me having not liked this isolation. However, I do also know school teachers who go to great effort to maintain parental contact, either by phone or in writing, and I recommend that you encourage this, as a parent's input and support is so vital to the young pianist (see chapter 8). Also, parents are the ones paying so they deserve to know how their offspring are progressing, or not.

A further option is to remain private but undertake to visit your pupils. This has the advantage of keeping your work and private life separate, and also affords you a better understanding of your students' playing as you will get to know the instrument and circumstances under which they are trying to learn. Sometimes this can be a noisy and busy house with the dog on the lap and baby sister crying in the corner. It's useful to know this sort of thing! You will have to be well organized though as there will be much time between lessons as you travel between students, and transporting all the relevant books becomes very hard work. And there will be times when the one book you need is at home in your cupboard!

I visited at the start of my teaching career but quickly found disadvantages. The aforementioned dog and baby were a reality, and it is very difficult to have autonomy in another person's house. I became frustrated carrying around a lot of music and did not like not having my whole library from which to choose sight-reading, aural, or new pieces. It was also very time consuming and I could not have taught so many students trying to get to each of their houses in a night. I have to say in addition that I always felt my students liked the whole experience of their lesson at my house. It was boundaried but friendly and, for a short time each week, their second home.

2. Getting Going

Now you know your potential student, how do you let them know of you?

Once you have decided that yes, piano teaching is what you want to do, and you have decided whom it is you would like to teach, you have to decide how to get them to know you exist.

Your marketing tool, as with the wording and placing of it, will depend on whom you are aiming at. Do you need flyers, posters for shop windows, business cards, small ads for the classifieds in music magazines or local papers, or maybe articles for local or specialized publications? And don't forget the internet. There are specialist sites where you can advertise your services, and you can also create your own website which becomes your 'shop front' and which you can make an individual and creative tool to advertise and market your business. And, of course, while the flyers and posters have to be brief, your website can expand on their content.

Whatever it is you decide, try to include something that will give prospective students or their parents a flavour of you as a person. In the final analysis, **a student or their parent will base their decision to come to you based on who you are and the relationship that you can build** with them/their offspring. The other issues will be important (training/qualifications/ background/ experience) but if a student does not click with you on some level its unlikely they will want to spend time with you, or listen to you, or do what you tell them.

It may seem like you have to write an essay to get people interested but even a business card can convey your character. I knew the importance of a logo as I'd worked in a marketing department for a large construction firm so I chose one that appeared on everything: card, flyers, posters, letters, and contracts. It was unusual, different, humorous, visible, and, importantly, appeared on *all* my literature- including the front of this book!. (NB, make sure there are is no copyright if you use one you haven't created.) No one used to mention this logo specifically until years into my teaching career a few people said how they had noticed it 'all over the place', and another noticed the 'humour' which had stood out for her. The comments I received started to reinforce what I'd instinctively felt; that it had helped to give me a highly unique and recognizable profile that people remembered when they were looking for a teacher.

Marketing Documents/wording

As I said, you will first need to decide what type of documents you want to produce. At the very least you will need a business card to drop off where people can see it and pick it up. *....a highly unique and visible profile*
Don't assume they

will always bother, or have with them a pencil and paper, to take down your number from ads and posters.

Your website, to which you will direct interested parties, will outline your experience and background, and also the specific qualities, strengths and characteristics that you bring to the lessons. You can emphasize any particular strands that you offer – like jazz, festival coaching, accompanying (for either auditions or exams), and improvising, and expand on the information outlined on your flyers and advertisements.

Try getting yourself mentioned in articles in the local paper. This way you create a personal and local focal point and can reach people who may not even know they are interested in lessons until they read about them. Posters and a website are there for people to find, this way you find them.

The wording and style of all your material is paramount. All is an expression of you, and will help attract the type of person you want. All your prose needs to be to the point, but still target your potential student; choose to be either creative, or more businesslike, or maybe 'cool', if aimed at the older teenager who is looking to go on to a music career. You can emphasize that you cover all aspects of the piano and music, or pick an area that you want to concentrate on, or better still, choose the wording depending on where you will place the ad.

If you are creating a poster or flyer then obviously the visual content has to have an instant appeal. You don't want people to have to read a book to learn about what you do and what you are offering. And one image can capture more than long paragraphs, as can the type of font/colouring/graphic layout. Keep it informative but keep it short and to the point.

Always try to make yourself stand out above the crowd. It can be anything from your amazing concert background, competition results, qualifications, or approach. Or, the layout of your advert which you can produce to ensure it catches people's eyes above your competitors. Piano teachers are a friendly and supportive group and will pass on pupils if they know that another teacher can offer something they can't for a particular student, but in the first instance you need the phone calls.

c Alexandra Westcott 2012

Find a niche in the market where you can capture a stream of the type of students that you teach. For instance, Mothers' coffee mornings or school magazines that go to the parents for youngsters; or for more advanced students, the school scholarship magazines.

Sometimes you just have to be in the right place at the right time. I knew a music teacher who, through one recommendation to a famous singer went on to became very famous. She was already a great teacher but the lucky contact put her well on the road. Most of us need to work at finding the clients that keep us doing what we love for a living.

I advertised everywhere until after a few years word of mouth basically kept new students coming. This will undoubtedly happen for you too, but at the start don't be afraid to put your name around as much as possible. And don't be afraid to take some poorly paid or free work; these will still serve as marketing tools and get you and your services known.

Along with word of mouth recommendations, don't forget exam and festival successes; these are all the most important factors that will make you stand out as a good teacher.

3. Administration

It is worth having most of your administration in writing. Then there are no arguments about lesson times, fees, rearrangements of lessons or term dates. I have gone through various methods of billing and informing my students' parents of dates/fees etc. Some professional bodies stress having an individual bill for each student itemizing the first lesson of term, the last, the cost of each lesson, the total cost of the term's lessons, and any additional fees. I used to do this, along with a newsletter in which I published my students' exam results, concert dates, term dates and anything else I wanted to say, until I realized that the bills never got read. It took an enormous amount of work so I now put the term's fees and dates on the newsletter, which gets sent out well before the end of each term, and which generally does get read. The only time I write a formal letter is to increase the fees.

.....have your contract in writing

A contract is not something every teacher has but it has proved invaluable to me, both as a means to focus a prospective students' parents/adult students on my terms and conditions, and as a legal reminder I am owed notice of discontinuing lessons. Sadly, a couple of times, I have had to use this legal obligation as a means by which to retrieve income when a parent has stopped lessons without notice. Most people will respect and understand that teaching the piano is your means of living, i.e. paying the bills. Some, however, won't, so it is clearer all round to have it in writing and you will attract a clientele who understand and respect your boundaries. I have refused to teach some people who have argued about missed lessons before they have even started. Some people seem to think we teach because we love it (we do) and don't realize that we also do it to pay the bills. They have no problem paying for a term's ballet or swimming but seem to think we are doing it in our spare time (most of the teachers I know rely solely on their teaching profession for their income). So, beware; if they don't agree with your terms and conditions then the relationship is off to a very dodgy start. After the first one or two dicey moments I didn't have any trouble, so my advice is to be clear from the start. You may lose a couple of prospective students but you want to put your energy into teaching, not arguing your conditions or worrying about where the next cheque is coming from!

I strongly advise joining a professional body of musicians – either the Musician's Union or the Incorporated Society of Musicians. Both can offer you standard contracts that you can use yourself, or they will help you word your own. They are there if you ever find yourself in a dispute and both provide a multitude of services that are invaluable as well as opportunities for networking and meeting colleagues.

4. Interviews

It is strongly advisable to meet your student and their parents before you both commit to signing a contract. It is an opportunity for you to check that it is the student who wants to learn for themselves and not the parent who is pushing it. It is also the time for you to outline your terms and conditions to the parent; and for the child to meet you and make sure they feel comfortable with you and your house. If you want to you can make it an audition, or check

put your energy into teaching

their musical aptitude, but I never did as I wanted to give anyone who wanted to learn the chance to do so. For some of the interview, focus your attention entirely on the child so as to make a connection with them, and to make sure that they understand that they will be required to work between lessons. Then, if you feel confident that they aren't being forced into it by the parent, offer them lessons. The parent can then go away with the contract to check over the details themselves and think about it, before committing to you.

One point about the child at the initial interview is that you may notice behaviour at this stage that you would not tolerate in a student. However, a young child is very different away from their parents; the child most buoyant at the interview can be much quieter on his/her own with you, and the child who is shy with his parents can quickly open up when alone with another adult. And talent and commitment, or lack of it, doesn't necessarily show up in a the first meeting, or audition. Even the most enthusiastic student may turn out to have no staying power, or real commitment. Hence, while it's worth making mental notes of how they are at the initial meeting, its always worth giving prospective students a chance.

5. The lessons

So, you have your students. Now what?

All teachers have their own ideas of what's important; of what order to teach things, and how to teach them, and I expect you already have a very good idea of how you intend to go about it. You may already have your first lesson plans, as I did, for the perfect ten first lessons. Unfortunately, there is no such thing as a 'perfect' pupil – i.e. the one that will fit those lessons - and you will probably quickly realize (as I did!) that those plans have to go out the window in favour of what's appropriate for each individual student. Of course it's this unknown that keeps us on our toes, keeps us creative, and keeps the work enjoyable.

I offer my suggestions after years of playing and teaching simply as a resource of ideas that you might like to dip into when inspiration deserts. They are based on years of questioning what I was taught, and are either repeating those things that worked, or resolving to offer different than those that did not. You will see that for the very young student there are a lot of activities that may seem to have nothing to do with music but engender other creative activities (writing, drawing). This is because music is an expressive art and you need to have ideas of what you are expressing. If I can encourage a student to feel inquisitive about what the music is saying, or depicting, then in the long run it will keep them curious as to what their own music is trying to express.

As a final point, from the beginning, all students should have a homework notebook in which you write their homework, and manuscript paper for theory/note writing etc.

Lesson 1 for a very young beginner

Having said that I no longer try to follow '10 first lessons', I do still follow a similar format for teaching the first lesson. I have a grand piano so I make the most of it by showing the child inside and letting them discover how it actually makes the sound. They are usually really excited to find out, and to play such a large impressive instrument.

Next we discuss the pattern of black and white notes and ascertain which notes of the alphabet are used, and then, as the easiest white key to locate, we learn to find D on the keyboard. Following this is finger numbers, posture and technique, and a song that they can take home and learn with finger numbers. I give them very simple finger exercises and finish the lesson with some listening games. Depending on the amount of time left over I play a selection of the following: nursery rhymes for them to guess; music for them to describe as walking running, marching or skipping; and clapping and copying. I don't worry too much about the answers except in as much as it gives me an idea of their aural and rhythmic ability. The most important thing is NOT TO LET THE STUDENT FEEL STUPID. It's paramount that they feel comfortable with trying out answers and not worrying if they are wrong. For a lot of the time I try not to tell them an answer is 'incorrect'. If they think 2/4 sounds like skipping, then to them perhaps it does. Later you can guide them towards the more usual answer!

I have devoted a large section to Parental Help but I will just say here that at the end of the first lesson I spend some time showing the parents the technical points. Not just how it looks but how it feels and why it is important. I explain what to do, how to do it, and show them the logic behind it and where it will lead (ie a technique that will serve whatever music they learn to love and want to play). The parents are the ones at home while the child develops his/her habits so it is vital at this stage that these habits are going to be good ones! (Check the section about 'Practice'). I also explain everything that we have covered in the lesson and what I expect the pupil to learn over the week ahead.

Finding the White Notes on the piano

Although I explain that we use the first 7 letters of the alphabet to describe the notes in music, I use the pattern of black and white notes right from the beginning to teach where the individual notes sit on the keyboard.It can be quite a long time before I show that they climb the alphabet consecutively. If you are wondering why, it's because I have had experience of a pupil at Grade 5 who still had to climb from C to find G!

I point out the groups of three and two black notes and get the child to find them with their eyes shut, (harder than you think!), before naming D as the white between the two black notes. Then they have to find it for themselves, first with their eyes open then with their eyes shut, and at different times during the lesson we go back to this. The first song we play

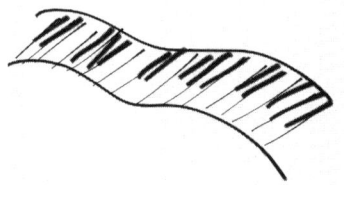

has finger two on D so by the end of week one they certainly know this. Then over the course of the next few weeks I teach B and F, and then C and E, before teaching to name any consecutive notes. We continually go back to this for as long as it takes, quite some time for some of them. Even after they start playing the notes from the manuscript they can still find locating random notes tricky. You can invent your own games, and more are listed in Appendix i.

Technique

It's extremely hard to describe in writing such a physical aspect of the piano but as it is often so badly taught, or ignored, I think it is worth trying.

I have had the enormous fortune to be taught by Nelly Ben Or, the top Alexander Technique teacher in the UK, who is also a renowned concert pianist. She has spent 40 years looking at piano playing in the light of the philosophy and attitudes of F M Alexander and it provides the most remarkable approach to the piano, developing a deep sense of logic and clarity, freedom and mindfulness. If you don't know much about it then I suggest an exploration for yourself as it's the sort of thing that's hard to put into words, but I will try, and if nothing else it might inspire you to investigate further.

Technically it is often about what we *don't* do rather than what we *do* do. An adult once described it as the 'Zen' of piano playing! This is a good description. A piano key weighs about 2oz yet the strain that many pianists place on their whole body just to depress this weight is enormous! All that is needed is a release of energy, from the fingertip, directly down into the key. If a student is sitting straight then no muscles are used in holding the back up as the vertebrae are balanced, and the arms can be supported from the solidity of the back rather than the tension of the biceps or triceps. The body isn't *made* to sit in any position, but just allowed to find this natural supported posture. Arms

should be supported and light and not sagging at the side – this provides a very heavy constraint on any velocity or lightness and ease of flow. A young student pointed out that it was like 'first position for the arms in Ballet'. This is a great description; I found that even students who did not learn ballet knew what I meant and lengthened their arms and opened up their chest when prompted by this.

velocity, lightness and ease of flow

The action of depressing the key is a tiny but precise and sensitive release of energy through just the fingertip. The rest of the hand is loose and unstrained and the finger depressing the key returns to this unstrained group of muscles within a split second of playing the note. It is very similar to switching an electric light switch of the rocker type.

You will have your own exercises for technique but I will mention some here, which are very much aimed at isolating the issues at hand (pun intended!).

It is vital that the fingers involved in depressing the note remain unstrained. It is very interesting to rest the keys on the piano lid and just 'feel' the lid with each finger tip. You will immediately notice if the other fingers fly up, or if the fingers lift *up* before going down, or after coming up. All of which is unnecessary and engenders a build up of tension and strain that is not conducive to fluid and even runs.

Once on the keys I get a student to play repeated notes, slowly paying attention to *letting* the other fingers remain unaffected (holding them down is as bad as holding them up!), and also to *allowing* the weight of the note to raise their finger back, as opposed to lifting the finger.

A few lessons later (or how ever long it takes before I think they are ready) I explain 'walking' from 1-2 or 2-3. This is done in the same way with the same attention. I don't encourage legato at this point unless it comes naturally as for little ones who find it difficult it creates great strain, and all manner of undesirable compensations (mostly in the wrists).

As it is about developing habits, short very focused bursts are better than long protracted sessions with concentration slipping.

c Alexandra Westcott 2012

Thumbs are a problem for pianists and are where a lot of the tension in technique is created. The impetus for the movement comes right from the tip. The rest of the hand is left quietly alone. Showing a young student how the thumb 'leaves' the hand (opens up from it) will encourage them not to tighten the muscles and 'attach' it, as it were, to the first finger. This in turn can either result in, or be the result of, using the wrist to bang the thumb down, or 'rocking' the hand towards the thumb so that the thumb, in effect, isn't what is playing the note. The problem has to be approached from both possible causes. Showing them how the tip can slide across the notes and under the hand to reach the little finger is a good way to show the extent of movement the thumb has, and then independent notes depressed with the thumb alone can be tried, of course at all times paying close attention to the rest of the hand.

Later on playing C and C# with the thumb and 3rd finger and all the other fingers resting loosely close together without any wrist movement or tension will indicate further if the movement of the thumb has been understood, and if not, is another good exercise for remedying it. Once scales are introduced, first get the student to play C, F, C, F with the RH thumb (CGCG with the LH thumb) before including the intervening notes.

'*Practice*'

There are many things about 'practice' which involve discipline, but try to encourage your students' to see it as something motivated by eager enthusiasm and a desire to play and learn rather than motivated by guilt or dread. This change of perception will raise their attitude, and therefore their study, to a different level of quality. At all times, a student should be acquiring the skill of '*getting* it right', not '*putting* it right'. (Christopher Bunting)

You notice I use practice in parenthesis. This is because actually I veer away from the word practice as much as possible. A couple of the many dictionary definitions are 'habitual performance', and 'repeated or systematic exercise'. You cannot do either unless you KNOW what it is you are doing! So a session at the piano is about LEARNING until such a time when KNOWING is reached. Then follows playing, and perfecting, both with a curious and enquiring mind. At no time do I advocate unmindful repeated 'drilling'. All time spent at the piano should have attention and concentration so as to incur clarity of the text and freedom of muscles. (See my article on Piano Playing and the Alexander Technique). Unmindful practice does not make perfect, unless you can include perfect mistakes and a perfectly awful technique! Engaging absorbing and attentive study at the piano makes perfect, takes a lot less time, and is a darn sight more interesting along the way!

6. Activities

...it keeps them engaged

Of course aurals and sight-reading are not games but call them such and it keeps the enthusiasm and energy high. Some of them make up an integral part of a lesson and learning a piece, while others offer light relief at the end of the lesson. As far as the student is concerned, especially the younger ones, they are guessing games. Of course I hope that they are using their ear/initiative/knowledge and don't guess but they don't have to know that! They are aimed at encouraging a creative and curious and enquiring ear, as well as an accurate ear. You will notice that some of them are quite physical (running up and down the room to find notes, for instance) – this is a very good way to keep the whole thing lively and also prevent loss of concentration, especially for the much younger learner!

I have introduced many games over the years and outline the most popular and useful. Make sure that when possible they get to be the 'leader' too. It keeps them engaged in the 'game' and prevents them from feeling that they are always being tested. And it's much more fun when things are interactive.

Much of these are aimed at the young beginner or young student, but many of them can continue, either as indicated or adapted, for the older or more advanced player.

1   For finding notes on the piano:

- Play groups of 3/2 black notes with eyes shut (this develops a 'feel' for the geography of the keyboard
- Run round the room coming back to a named note
- Play white notes with eyes shut (using the black groups as a guide)
- Spell words using the notes on the piano – make it more fun by telling a story
- Jump up all the …..e.g. 'G's – make it more fun by finding words that begin with the letter

2   For development of rhythm:

- Clapping and copying (let them be the 'leader' too) – this develops their listening and memory

a feel for pulse......

- Clapping nursery rhymes – both of you together, and then separately as a 'guess the nursery rhyme from the rhythm' game - this distinguishes whether they can tell the rhythm from the pulse and develops a tight and accurate sense of rhythm (you would be surprised at how many young students, at the beginning, don't clap all the syllables).
- Marching/Skipping/Swaying in time to the music – this develops a feel for pulse,
- Clapping the pulse in time to the music – you can make this interesting by asking them to pretend to cut a hedge and cutting high up when the music goes higher, and lower when the music is lower etc. – this develops their feel for pulse (and pitch). If they cannot seem to locate

c Alexandra Westcott 2012

the pulse by clapping ask them to tap their foot. This seems to be much more instinctive than clapping. Then, when their foot is tapping the beat, you can suggest they clap along with it.

- Clap a short piece while the student watches the music. Make a 'mistake' and get them to tell you where and what it is – this tests and develops their intuition for comparing what they hear with what they see on the page

an accurate and perceptive ear.....

3   *For developing pitch (some of these may not seem to test or develop anything but in fact they will be encouraging an accurate and perceptive ear)*

- 'Guess which note is higher' (Start with them far apart then get closer)

- Play notes and ask: Going Up or down? - in very little young children they might never have come across the concept of high or low sounds, or what they sound like, or which end of the instrument is which

- Similar to the hedge cutting game, play music and suggest they pretend they are picking blackberries; having to pick higher when the music is high, and lower when the music goes down

- You sing and they sing back - this develops their aural memory

- You play and they sing back – this develops aural memory

- You play while they are not watching and they play back (keep this very simple – use one note and vary the rhythm or dynamic at first, then add one note etc – it will depend on the student how far you can take this) – this is a very good aural test which develops memory, an accurate ear, and has them representing on the piano what they hear.

- Guess the nursery rhyme (this time from the tune)

- Guess the step/skip/5th/octave etc – if done in tandem with recognizing intervals on the stave then it will help with aural and visual recognition

- Play a melodic interval and see if they can chose one note to sing, then the other. Later on you can get them to sing from one to the other and ask the interval. Do the same with a harmonic interval..much harder!

- Play them a note while they shut their eyes and ask them to sing it. See if they can find it on the piano - this is good to help them with recognizing sounds and pitch and also memory as they have to retain the first note to be able to match it

- As above but this time play a short melody of a few notes (vary depending on age/ability/standard)

- Sing Scale passages up and down

- Play a tonic, play a further note of the same scale and ask them to sing up to it and name the interval

- As above but without singing the intervening notes.

- Place the student's fingers over the same five notes as yours, then play a couple of bars and they copy, (I often use the start of the blues scale with this, but you can also use a diatonic scale) firstly with eyes open, then by ear with eyes shut. Start with a rhythm on one note then add one note at a time. I do this with blues and play a whole round of 12 bars while playing just a varied rhythm on one note in the RH. Then I add the next note for 12 bars, then the third etc. They are surprisingly good at copying this. Let them have a go at playing the two bars while you copy. This introduces them to improvising as well as aural.

- [W] Dictate a rhythm or melody for them to write down. Keep it simple!

4   *For note recognition on the Stave/sight-reading/memory*

- [W] Lots of writing and naming notes

- [W] Flash cards – put the cards in a pile at the opposite end of the room and get them to run to the pile, pick a card, run back to the piano and play it, get another card etc. Time them!

- [W] Spell words using the notes on the flash cards

- [W] Clap an easy piece naming the notes in time to the rhythm

- [W] Name the notes of a piece to a metronome – one note per tick (so not following the written rhythm) with no pausing. If a note is unknown, move on. If they get muddled, they continue looking at one note per tick of the metronome until they are calm enough and can continue naming. This forces the brain to learn to think quickly, and not to hesitate over unknown or wrong notes, necessary for sight-reading. If time is always given to work out a note then the brain never learns to speed up.

- [W] Glance at a bar then play from memory – one hand or both depending on age and ability

- [W] The pupil watches the music while you play and tells you where you are on the page when you stop

- ☒ The pupil watches an easy piece as you play it and spots the 'mistake' - this is another one for developing their ability to recognize what they hear with what they see

- ☒ Sight-reading a piece but missing out every repetition of a chosen note while leaving the correct rhythmic space for it (this is surprisingly tricky, especially if doing a note in both hands at the same time!)

- ☒ Give them 30" to look at a line of music then cover it up – how much can they remember (clef/key/time signature/first notes/expression marks)

- ☒ Put one hand on the black notes and one hand on the white then play through the rhythm only of a piece. This takes the emphasis away from the right notes and the (fairly awful) noise gets them used to strange sounds, which is sometimes what holds them up from playing in time when sightreading.

5   General Activities

- ☒ 'Grandma's Basket'. A good one for extending memory. You play one note. They play it and add another, random, note. You play both and add another. They play all three and add another, etc. This is excellent for memory. I got to over 150 notes with one student – though be warned, it took us a couple of hours! It also develops the ability to see notes as 'groups' as it's impossible to remember all the notes as one-off random notes. The brain is forced to put them into groups of recognizable patterns. Later on when they are memorizing music using harmonic progressions they are already used to consolidating groups of notes into single 'items'.

- [x] Ask the student to draw to a piece of music – or write a story/make up a title. This develops the idea that music is expressive and that it can also be descriptive. (you can use a piano piece or orchestral CD)

- [x] Ask the student to describe the features of a piece of music – either played on the piano or an orchestral piece on a CD – they can range from simple musical directions (crescendo/accelerando etc?) to more elaborate or in depth

- [x] Find 3 descriptive or emotive words to fit a piece (use various pieces, including but not only the ones they are learning. With their own pieces, ask them to make sure they are conveying the words they have chosen when they play it).

- [x] Draw repeating patterns or shapes to accompany repeated rhythms and motifs – and vice versa

- [x] Play music to describe a picture (free improvisation – although some of them will want to use scales and chords, you are going for the mood and atmosphere and energy of the picture without the concern of 'right' notes)

- [x] Find music of different periods and ask questions/discuss the instruments, sounds, rhythms etc. (A&C Black do a very good series called 'History of Music' – there are 3 books aimed at different ages. They have accompanying CDs and suggestions for activities and questions. They are aimed at groups but there are certainly some useful things you can do with your instrumental student). Alfred Publishing also do extremely good books, one for each period (Baroque, Classical, Romantic and Modern), which include a CD of all the pieces, and tremendous but easy to read and understand information about the period, composer, ornamentation, alongside the politics and cultural happenings etc.

- With more advanced students try playing random notes but play them in a musical style or period – get the student to try and guess the period.

- Clap rhythms and get the student to make up words

6   Hide and seek

- This is the game that I made up with my first six year old pupil and has become a firm favourite – even with older students with whom you can make it more complicated! You hide a small object and instead of using the 'hot and cold' way to direct the seeker, you use high and low, or loud and soft, fast and slow, major and minor, different pieces, etc. You get the idea. Vary it and let them chose which is 'hot' and which is 'cold'.

7   For Harmony

- As soon as the student can understand and play their first scale, and are ready to learn the second, I teach the primary triads. From this we can improvise in a number of styles, and increase the memorizing of pieces.

8   For Memorizing

- From the very early days I get the pupil to play their short pieces with their eyes shut. Later we take a simple piece (maybe one of the number 12's from Edna Mae Burnham's Dozen a Day) and discuss it, then play it straight away without the music, so that they start to learn how to play from a clear and intelligent perspective rather than muscle memory. Of course the fingers need to learn passages, but there has to be an underlying clarity and understanding otherwise a one time awkward reaction becomes a habitual response that creates tension and stiffness. (For more on this refer to the chapter on Technique, and also my article on my experiences on the Alexander Technique that go into more detail).

- I have arranged memory workshops for students to play to each other a piece learnt entirely from memory. We spend the lesson directly before the workshop memorizing a small piece, discussing it and reciting it but without ever playing it. At the end of the same week the students come together on a Saturday afternoon and perform their pieces to each other from memory. This gives them a direct experience of how to memorize, which in turn increases their confidence of performing – pieces are much less likely to go wrong if memorized this way, as opposed to when relying solely on muscle memory. If there is a slip, it can be recalled from the mind, rather than the performer having to start right back at the beginning, hoping that this time their fingers will carry them through. It is also a first introduction to musical analysis that makes it relevant to the student.

9   For Improvising (see also scale section)

- As mentioned above, we do lots of 'free' improvising – often using pictures as a prompt for the imagination. This means the sounds of the piano can be enjoyed and explored without the worry of 'right notes'. Very early beginners can use the pedals, glissandi (they will find a way!), clusters etc that they wouldn't otherwise encounter for many years in the pieces.

- Make up some 'happy/sad etc' music – using free improvisation or scales and chords

- Even if not a jazz musician, blues is excellent for improvising as it so conveniently uses the primary triads of a scale that a student is already learning. It also sounds very effective very early on. My students and I take turns to play the top and the bass and we vary whether we play straight or swing. It's an obvious time to introduce different scales, for instance the blues or pentatonic scales in a way that makes them relevant. Sometimes we play question and answer and other times we take a whole part each. I also use blues as a question and answer aural (see above).

10   Theory

[W] The theory and writing down of music is an important part of a musical education so I encourage you to include it from the start. Make it interesting and relevant to their pieces and their interests (maybe they like writing songs). There are now some wonderful books for young children that include colour and stickers to make what can be a dry subject very entertaining. In the early stages the writing of notes helps with the learning and understanding of the stave.

11   For *Scales*

From the earliest stages – get the students to play all their scales using each note as a starting note (so for the scale of C, they go from C-C, D-D, E-E etc). This has a huge number of benefits that become apparent as time goes on, not least as they start to see the geography of the key and not just the linear pattern of the scale. It also means they will have covered the minor mode without any trouble, and, should they continue to learn jazz, the other modes too.

Then get them to play *with* the scales. ie playing them in different rhythms, dynamics etc. This gets a student inside a key in a creative fashion, rather than getting stuck on what can seem an irrelevant string of notes. It is also a 'safe' way into improvising as there is the boundary of repetition and scale.

Ask a student to accompany themselves playing a RH scale with a LH chord, for example chords I and IV (in second inversion) on the first and 5th RH notes (which are played as quavers. See ex. 1)) Going on from this they can then continue the chord pattern and improvise with the scale.

This is a good way of introducing a scale as a whole landscape rather than a string of notes. Playing a syncopated rhythm ups the challenge (ie on quaver beats one and 4. See ex 2).

ex 1.

RH ♫♫♫♫
LH x   x

ex 2.

RH ♫♫♫♫
LH x x

Following this I use the same chord shapes but include V7b, using the progression I, IV, V, I etc. Once they have mastered the changing chords we turn them into an Alberti bass using the same inversions and progressions. This is very good practice in preparation for the classical repertoire and bringing creativity to the world of technique, scales and harmony.

7. Additional Motivational pursuits

Exams

These provide an excellent benchmark and motivation for students who are enjoying their piano and want to feel a sense of progress and achievement. BUT, they certainly do not suit all students and should never be forced, or be the total syllabus of a students' work.

The Associated Board has written a wonderful book about them,'These Music Exams', which is provided free either at your local music shop or from the AB. It describes how a student can prepare for an exam, and how a teacher and parent can support that candidate so that the exam is a positive experience. And its worth remembering, the examiners are not there to sit in judgement but to provide an experienced and guiding ear and advice on a musical journey.

Pupils' Concerts

I have organized these twice a year since I started teaching. The benefits and rewards are great both for the students and their parents. .....inspiration all round

Whether or not a student wants to take exams, having a concert gives them a goal to aim for and preparing to perform, and performing, will not only take a students' playing to another level but gives a huge sense of achievement after the end of the event.

For parents, it provides an ongoing record of achievement as over the years they see the level of progress attained by each piece. I have all the students play so that they can hear a variety of music and standards. It provides inspiration and encouragement all round.

Some teachers limit the audience to the other students; others have their exam candidates play to each other in preparation for an exam. All of these events can have their place over a teaching year.

Having decided on the format you have to find a location. Over the years I have housed concerts in my own home; at local schools with private theatres, complete with raked seats and lighting; country houses, and local churches. On top of an excellent piano, raked seating used to be of high importance so that the smaller members of the families could see, but it became increasingly difficult to find places that accommodated my numbers and offered the other facilities I wanted (space for tea, enough room for all the players and their families, locality and parking) at a price I could afford. So, having avoided churches, for the simple reason that I wanted to provide a concert hall experience for my students, I finally felt that the deciding factors had to be the piano, room for a party, and enough space to accommodate extended families. For years I settled on a local church that has the most wonderful Steinway grand and that housed us perfectly and at

a very reasonable cost, for years. I would pay a couple of the older students to help me which gave them a sense of responsibility and they enjoyed being involved.

Decide if, how much, and who you will charge. You will obviously want to cover the costs but you can do this either by charging an overall cost per player that includes whomever they want to bring, or charging individual ticket prices for performers and audience alike, or just charging the audience. I never charged the performers as I felt the concert was provided for them, but I charged the parents. You may decide to make enough to donate to a charity. You may open the concert to the public. I went against this latter idea as I wanted the concert to be a safe environment for my students to experience performing, without added judgement from outsiders who, having paid, would have been expecting perfect performances. My performers ranged from 4 year olds playing Mary Had a Little Lamb to adults who hadn't played the piano before, let alone in public, to Grade 8 students who had developed aplomb for performing, and I wanted them all to feel the warmth of a supportive audience.

Even after the smaller concerts that took place in my house, I offered refreshment, from tea and cake, with a larger party and mulled wine at the Christmas concert, complete with presents and decorations. The relief, excitement and buzz following a performance needs an outlet and it gives the parents, students, and extended members of the family to talk to each other, and of course you!

Visits to professional concerts

Over the years I have organized concert visits for my students and their parents. Apart from being able to acquire more competitive ticket prices, it is sometimes a necessary motivation for people who may want to attend such events but are so busy arranging their lives they don't get around to arranging concerts. And of course it's nice to know that your students are listening to quality music that, hopefully, they will want to emulate.

Theory workshops/game afternoons.

I run these afternoons for about 10/12 of students of a similar standard and hand out a crib sheet beforehand outlining the information that they need to know. Then we play musical bingo/pictionary or hangman. I've also done a (very complicated!) treasure hunt during which they had to collect notes – all of which were described in various ways but that when entered on a large stave made a tune. It was fun. You can think of your own ideas.

Memorizing workshops – see above

Competitions- if these are your thing (I have mixed feelings about them) then there are a number of avenues:

Composing competitions run by yourself for your students. (I got a fellow teacher and a non musician to judge together which was very interesting and gave a two dimensional result)

Scale competitions within your students

Local musical competitions and festivals

8. Parental contact/help

This is vital for young students – or basically any student who is not yet paying for their own lesson. Hopefully the more advanced teenage students will have got into a rhythm of learning but, sadly, this isn't always the case. Parents should keep an eye on the time spent at the piano, and as a teacher I always keep in very close touch with the parent. My relationship with the student is first and foremost and if they are not fulfilling their commitment I will talk to them first, but (and depending on the age this is sooner or later) I will also pass on my concerns to the parent. Mostly they are very grateful. Unfortunately there are some who just don't have the time to devote to their children's musical life and this means some tough decisions from you. I have been very sad that some students have failed to manage the challenges of the piano, not because of their own lack of enthusiasm, but primarily because they didn't have the support at home.

Learning music should be fun to do but there are processes along the way that can seem like an uphill struggle, especially to a young beginner. If these are persevered though, a student will gain more freedom at the instrument and, therefore, *more* fun and a greater ability to express him or herself, which is why they come to the piano in the first place. After a number of years teaching it became very apparent just how fundamental parental support is to the development of a student's progress, not just with regards how far that student will go, but even whether they will get off the starting block or not.

Parents can do much to harness their child's enthusiasm for music, encouraging a positive progress to emerge as a result of curiosity and fun, rather than slog and boredom

Parental involvement - Why and how?

It may seem obvious to suggest that a parent facilitates its child's learning but it doesn't always happen, and it is vital that with so many after school activities the student is assisted in finding a regular time to fit their piano playing into their schedule. On top of this, as a solo instrument, learning the piano can sometimes feel lonely and isolating for a very young beginner, so having the encouragement and close proximity of a parent can be a positive support to their experience. The time at home is also the time when technical habits are learned and ingrained, so having an extra eye and ear keeps things on track.

Parental support doesn't have to make learning the piano seem like hard work. On the contrary, it can add a fun and interactive element to what can sometimes be a struggle in the early stages when there is so much new material to absorb and digest. Having a parent help schedule the time, and gently discipline the child to keep to this schedule, can be an enormous benefit when there are so many other distractions.

Music is an expressive and communicative art so a student needs to feel comfortable with themselves, and allowing them an inquisitive mind and lively ear, and the freedom to translate their expressions to sounds, is vital in their growth as musicians. It's challenging but necessary to encourage them without judgment so that they feel free to explore the colours and sounds of the instrument without feeling censored, but are guided in areas where there is a 'right' or 'wrong' (i.e. note).

Finally, I'm a great fan of rewards, but I think the rewards should be for trying rather than for getting it 'right'. Sometimes the road to getting things right is rather long so boosts along the way can give us the encouragement we need to continue to the end.

Frequently asked questions from parents about practice:
How Often?

This depends on the age of the child, their stage in learning, their own enthusiasm, their concentration span, and the quality of the practice. In the very early stages when the fundamentals are being absorbed, as long as there is an understanding of what is being learnt, then little and often is probably best. As things become more complex then a little more time is needed to reach a mental understanding of what is being learnt, and a correspondingly increasing amount of time is needed to physically absorb it into the fingers. I am of the mind that it is important to have days off built into a schedule so there are guilt free non-piano days, rather than schedule practice every day and then 'not get around to it', but at the same time I know for some students it works to have it so ingrained into their routine, like cleaning their teeth, that they come to the piano without question and just get down to their work. It works differently for different families so encourage them to find a structure that works for them.

How Long?

See above. The same constraints apply with regards age, standard, level of concentration etc. And it will be different for each student. In any case though, allow for periods of 'fiddling' and games on top of the homework that you set, either within the practice session, or maybe in a second daily session. For instance, covering the set practice in the morning then leaving the pupil to do whatever takes their fancy in the evening - improvising, games, messing about finding tunes etc. Ideally when new technical habits are being formed then even the fiddling should be mindful, otherwise the good work undertaken in the set time gets undone as old habits take over when concentration is elsewhere. However, paramount is an enthusiasm and curiosity for the music and instrument so it's up to a parents' judgment how much to intervene when a student is absorbed in his or her own world at the piano.

9. Holidays

In my view it is vital to have a break or two during the year to refresh and recharge your batteries. Whether you decide to do something completely different from music, do nothing at all, or just vary your workload is up to you, but I encourage you to have a change, and make some suggestions below.

Some students may not want such long breaks as the school holidays so you may decide to continue teaching and just enjoy the shorter hours. However, remaining available for only a few students can be uneconomical so bear this in mind.

You could offer short but intensive workshops with specific goals or aimed at a specific market. For instance, adult beginner workshops; workshops on the art of learning a piece; children's' general music and movement workshops; theory workshops; jazz workshops; master classes; or even residential weeks at one of the many locations around the country where students can really get absorbed in the subject on offer (any of the above could take place over a week's residential course). Of course you already have your student-base as a starting point for participants, so find what suits you and you will probably have no trouble getting it up and running.

Alternatively you may want to do something completely different than teaching which will give you a well earned break from the intensity of the profession but will bring in some income and new experience. Consider coaching for singers, for example, or accompanying instrumentalists or singers at an already established summer school.

...refresh and recharge your batteries

Without the demands of your teaching it is also a useful period to update your own study and let yourself get absorbed in learning new music, touching up your technique, or learning a new style. You may even consider attending a workshop yourself. I can highly recommend workshops; for a set period of time you can involve yourself completely in a subject that interests you (musical or not), which is impossible to do when trying to deal with the business of day to day life and work. Plus, you are with people of like mind and it's a wonderful way to make connections and friends of people with similar interests.

==Lastly, you could take a well earned rest and travel, or find a completely unmusical new hobby! Or all of the above, but whatever you do, find something that gives you renewed energy and enthusiasm for the new term.==

10. Ending lessons.

Hopefully this will, in the main, be when students finish their A levels and leave to go to University. However, there are other times that they will struggle and may well decide to stop. Entering senior school is one of them. Moving to another area or having too much else to do are two others. Of course you hopefully have your notice period mapped out and agreed so you will have time to fill the space vacated.

However, there will be times when a student is turning up for lessons but you are seriously wondering why?! I said at the beginning you needed the patience of a saint, but there comes a time where your integrity as a teacher is in question if you continue to accept money for teaching a student if there is no learning taking place. Some opinions state that if a student wants to continue to come then they must be getting something from you. I agree with that but if you are being paid for teaching them the piano then I have always had to question the ethics if that learning stops and you continue to take money. Plus, for me personally it makes me so frustrated that my mood is seriously affected (for the worse!) for following students.

It is one thing to be patient, but when every possible avenue (easier pieces, harder pieces, more homework, less homework, different styles) has been covered and there is still no practice/enthusiasm/progress, then you may want to have a serious conversation, first with the student, then with the parent, preferably with the student present. It has gone both ways with me. Sometimes a student has perked up, though often this has been short lived and we have ended up parting ways. Other times it has had the desired effect and has led to better communication and a real commitment on behalf of the student.

I had one young teenager who appeared completely disinterested, sullen, and did very little that I asked during her week at the instrument. I approached her and her mother about it and later had a very distraught parent on the phone who said that she didn't recognise the student that I had been describing. That her daughter was fired up after the lesson and used to relay what I had taught with real excitement and enthusiasm. She said her daughter was upset but that she wanted to continue. In the weeks that followed the student and I found a new communication; agreed on the areas that she felt she needed to work on, and not only did she go on to become a fine musician, taking O and A Level music, but we went on to become good friends.

> ....better communication and a real commitment

So, try everything, but don't be afraid to approach both the student and parent if you are concerned about progress. If you lose a student then you are making way for someone more committed, and just because you are not the right teacher for everyone doesn't mean you are not a good teacher, or the right teacher for someone else.

Where its all happened for 20 years...

Appendix i

Recommended Books/Resources

Tutors (I usually use three - two tutors and Dozen A Day - in tandem so that the material gets plenty of reinforcement)

Tunes for 10 Fingers - Pauline Hall - Pub by OUP
Dozen a Day - Edna Mae Burnham - Pub by Music Sales
Ministeps to Music - Edna Mae Burnham Pub by Willis Music
Me and My Piano - Fanny Waterman - Pub by Faber Music
Piano Magic - Jane Sebba - Pub by A&C Black

Theory

Theory Fun Factory 1-3 - Katie Elliot Pub by Boosey & Hawkes
My First Theory Book - Lina Ng - Pub by Rhythm
Theory Made Easy - Lina Ng - Pub by Rhythm
Theory Made Easy for very little Children - Lina Ng - Pub by Rhythm
Music Theory in Practice – ABRSM Pub by ABRSM

Aural

Aural Time - David Turnbull Pub by Music Sales
Aural Training in Practice - ABRSM Pub by ABRSM
Improve your Aural - Paul Harris Pub by Faber Music

Sight-reading

Improve Your Sight-reading)
Improve Your Practice   ) Paul Harris Pub by Faber
Let's read Music - Christine Brown (tactile note reading/learning resource good for young ages)
Joining the Dots - Alan Bullard Pub ABRSM

General

Music made Simple - Peter Diamond - possibly out of print but a really useful run through music history alongside the growth of notation and theory.

A history of piano masterworks – Alfred Music Publishing: a wonderful series containing a huge selection of pieces of a widely varying styles, and many of them little known, (some pieces crop up in every compilation – many of these don't) together with a very nicely played and recorded CD. It contains lots of information on the music and form and style of the period, together with the influence of society and its trends on the composers, and information specific to the composers and pieces in the book.

Your local music shop may have CDs and Books on composers and their lives aimed at children - great for long car journeys!

CDs of the exam pieces - I play the pieces through for a student to decide what they would like to learn but to have the music at home to listen to on a regular basis will imbue their ear with music played with expression and a good tone. Hearing you once a week is not enough, and without a guide to what a good sound is on the piano they can't be at fault for thinking that getting the notes right is enough.

Apps for the your smart phone or tablet

In this age of electronics there are a very large number of extremely good apps that develop sight reading skills, and also some for aiding theory or harmony explanations. I love them, as do my students.

Some I have on my phone and/or tablet are:

iReadmusic (excellent timed note reading in a variety of formats)
Read Music (theory testing game)
Aural Trainer (ABRSM aural training app)
PianoBird (really brilliant note naming game - FREE!)
Piano Reader by Wessar (Sightreading app - really excellent)
Theory - very well explained theory app
Chords and Scales - very visual app for all scales and chords
Autoflip (for page turning)

Organizations

It is worth checking local organizations for mutual support and advice. Below are some of the more well known ones in the UK.

ISM
EPTA
MU
ABRSM

Further reading on teaching piano

A Music Teacher's companion - Paul Harris Pub by OUP (covers all instruments)
The Art of Effective Piano Teaching - Dino Ascari Pub by AuthorHouse
Pianists at Play - Dan Elder Pub by Kahn & Averil (not a teaching book but an interesting selection of essays by pianists and composers on how technique has changed over the years)
Raising an amazing musician - ABRSM - lots of useful information for your students' parents.

Further reading on the Alexander Technique

Indirect Procedures - A Musician's Guide to the Alexander Technique - Pedro de Alcantara Pub by Clarendon Press (better read in conjunction with lessons)

Appendix ii

Piano Playing with reference to the Alexander Technique

This is an article that I wrote about my own transition from a limiting technique to one that feels much freer and more expressive. Hopefully your students won't have to take the journey as with your guidance they will have developed a brilliant and expressive technique, but I have included it by way of a reminder as to how important it is to give your students a good technical and musical grounding.

In search of clarity – a personal account.

This isn't about me. It's about how far one can travel given the right guide. But I have to tell you a little about my own piano playing to put my experience in context. I started learning the piano at 8 years old (38 years ago now) and loved it. I taught myself before being sent to a teacher and with his guidance quickly moved through the grades. But, and it's a big but, there was a limit to his guidance and I later realised that there was much material I would never master. My technique was ok but limited, as was my approach to the text, and I resigned myself to continuing my playing around the same level. Even when I returned to the piano as an adult and had lessons with a long standing local teacher, I couldn't see any way to advance my technique and she wasn't providing me with any answers.

I achieved a degree in Performing Arts, with music and recital as my major, and later built up a large successful teaching practice, but still felt there were areas that needed attention. I attended courses to develop both my teaching skills and my own playing and it was with great interest that I came across a course that combined the piano with the principles of the Alexander Technique. I had already come across the Alexander Technique, and was interested in it, but had no idea how it related to the piano, so it was with great curiosity that I booked and I haven't looked back since.

The course was run by Nelly Ben-Or and it was 15 years ago. Within moments I knew that she was something special and I could see that with her perspective a new world of possibilities at the piano opened up. I remember ringing my husband in the break in great excitement to tell him that I'd found something that I knew would change the way

I approached my piano. But, and this was what was so exciting, was that it was so obvious. And logical. Not weird or new age, just logical.

Nelly has been a concert pianist from the age of 13 and a teacher of the Alexander Technique for over 40 years. When she found the Technique she knew that it had something to offer far beyond the usual perception of 'how to sit down', stand or have a "correct" posture. After a few years of training to be an Alexander teacher she realised that she could start to use the principles of the Alexander Technique to help her assess her own preconceptions in piano playing.

The Alexander Technique goes way beyond our physical reactions, back to our deeply ingrained mental and physical responses, so it is to those that we need to look. Not in a soul searching and analytical way, but simply in a quiet and attentive way that most of us have gone beyond finding in our frantic day to day lives. Mostly we are too goal orientated, and don't stay present in the process of reaching the goal. So, existing tensions and awkward habits prevent achieving that goal. Finding a physical, mental and emotional stillness and clarity engenders the circumstances that enable us to have a free tactile contact with the instrument for a directness and depth of musical expression.

With reference to the piano then, it is about developing a new understanding of ourselves and our approach to the music and the instrument. What is less simple is undoing and letting go of our preconceptions, both physical and mental, that we have ingrained in us and that we feel keep us 'in control'.

Ah yes. Control. As in life, we think we have it when in fact we are at the mercy of all our automatic habits and reactions and the resulting tensions. To really learn the freedom that gives velocity and expression a voice at the piano we need to be a clear channel for our musical intention to become expressed in sound through an alert, free and sensitive contact with the keys. No complicated finger movement, arm weight, or some preconceived wrist action is necessary. But, and it's a big but, we have to be prepared to be constantly vigilant and interrogate our habits; to question, and then undo, the things that we have done without thinking for years. This needs a total attention to our ways of playing for it to happen, but if one is prepared to really engage with oneself and ones problems at the instrument, the answers come and the rewards are huge.

It took me years, and is and will continue to take many more, to let go of the tensions and physical and mental habits that I had acquired over the previous 20 or so years of piano playing. My automatic habitual 'will' still wants me to make short cuts, or tries to tell me that more is more, rather than to let go of being so busy and, literally go with the flow. (I don't need to tell you that I find it as hard to do this in life!). But I've reaped the benefits. With a more sensitive and available touch I can mould the music as I wish, rather than as the limits of my muscle capacity would allow. I learn much music away from the piano, which means I have the text, literally, at my fingertips, and therefore avoid the artificial technical obstacles that arise from some old ways of mechanical practicing and mental vagueness. Technical issues become a series of mentally worked out and clear components - 'beads'- that are strung together smoothly. Suddenly 'effortless' playing produces beautiful sounds, singing and flowing melodies, and fluid runs. The less I do, the more I can achieve.

Nelly has passed on her years of experience and profound wisdom to many, many pianists over the years on her courses. She receives grateful letters from professionals, students, teachers and gifted amateurs who have found this approach - based on her years of experience in applying principles of the Alexander Technique to so many aspects of piano playing – opening up unexpected new horizons in their music making. Usually what's in the way is only themselves. Once we get out of the way, then there is only the music. Isn't that what any musician wants?

Credits:

I have to credit my students and their parents from over 20 years teaching who have made the teaching and learning process so happy, creative and rewarding, and a place of mutual support and fun.

Also I offer grateful thanks to the organizations and individuals below from whom I have had so much advice and support over the years:

Tona West
Nelly Ben Or
ABRSM

Alexandra
Alexandra Westcott, BA
A Member of the ISM

alexandrawestcott@yahoo.co.uk
www.alexandrawestcottpiano.co.uk

7227441R00030

Printed in Great Britain
by Amazon.co.uk, Ltd.,
Marston Gate.